Delicious Dessert Cocktails

by Barbara Scott-Goodman

illustrated by Lauren Tamaki

Bluestreak
BOOKS

introduction

Welcome to the delicious world of dessert cocktails, the book for those who just can't decide whether to have a drink or dessert. It's simple—just have both!

Here is a collection of recipes to create and enjoy, from classic favorites to fun contemporary inventions, all year-round. What could be more festive to drink after dinner than a flute of Fresh Blueberry Prosecco on a spring evening, or more fun to serve for dessert at an outdoor barbecue than Margarita Ice Pops? On colder nights you and your guests will want to warm up and savor drinks like Amaretto Hot Chocolate and Classic Irish Coffee for dessert.

There are also number of easy recipes for bar basics like Simple Syrup and syrups flavored with ginger, spices, and fresh herbs that are sure to bring an extra level of flavor and depth to your cocktails.

In addition there are recipes for light desserts like Chocolate Meringues, Strawberries and Cream, and Port-Roasted Figs that are elegant, sumptuous, and easy to prepare.

From traditional cocktails to new and inventive libations, *Delicious Dessert Cocktails* delivers spirited dessert drinks that are decadent, luxurious, and, yes, delicious.

Cheers!

a word about measurements

Many professional bartenders use a little cup called a jigger to determine how much of a spirit to pour into a cocktail. In the United States most of the jiggers hold one-and-a-half ounces of liquid; in other parts of the world a jigger may hold a little less or a little more.

Because the jigger and its loyalty to ounces encourages many book authors to rely on the ounce to designate the amount of liquor needed for a favorite bar drink, many drinks recipes are written in ounces.

Not so in this book. Here the recipes are written in standard American measurements: teaspoons, tablespoons, and cups. This should make it easy for both the nervous host and the more seasoned one to pour their dessert cocktails with certainty.

If you want to translate the recipes into ounces, that's fine, too. Just follow this guide:

1 tablespoon = ½ ounce
2 tablespoons = 1 ounce
½ cup = 4 ounces
¾ cup = 6 ounces
1 cup = 8 ounces

chapter 1

BAR BASICS

~~~~~~~~~~~~~~~~~~~~~~~~~~~~~~~~

SIMPLE SYRUP

Simple Syrup is a mixture of sugar and water and is an important addition to all kinds of drinks. It's very easy to prepare and because it keeps well, is always good to have on hand in the refrigerator. Most simple syrup recipes call for one part sugar to one part water, but feel free to experiment with different ratios to come up with your preferred version (see page 11).

1 cup sugar

1 cup water

Put the sugar and water in a small saucepan and bring to a gentle boil over medium-high heat, stirring to dissolve the sugar. Reduce the heat and simmer, stirring occasionally, until the sugar is completely dissolved and the syrup is slightly thickened, about 3 minutes.

Remove from the heat and let cool. Transfer the syrup to a container with a tight-fitting lid, cover and refrigerate until ready to use. The syrup will keep, covered, in the refrigerator for up to 3 or 4 weeks.

Makes about 1 cup

~~~~~~~~~~~~~~~~~~~~~~~~~~~~~~~~

simple syrup ratios

Thick Simple Syrup: 1 part water to 1 part sugar

Medium Simple Syrup: 2 parts water to 1 part sugar

Thin Simple Syrup: 3 parts water to 1 part sugar

HONEY SIMPLE SYRUP

Many bartenders use honey simple syrup to add to whiskey, scotch, and bourbon cocktails. It also adds a lovely smooth flavor to hot and iced tea. The syrup is prepared like classic simple syrup with honey swapped in for the sugar.

1 cup honey

1 cup water

Put the honey and water in a small saucepan and stir. Bring to a gentle boil over medium-high heat, stirring constantly, until the honey is completely dissolved.

Remove from the heat and let cool. Transfer the syrup to a container with a tight-fitting lid, cover and refrigerate until ready to use. The syrup will keep, covered, in the refrigerator for up to 2 weeks.

Makes about 1 cup

GINGER SIMPLE SYRUP

Fresh ginger adds a nice aromatic kick to this simple syrup. It blends beautifully with lemonade and iced tea as well as bourbon and whiskey.

1 cup of sugar

½ cup water

Four 1-inch pieces fresh ginger, trimmed and peeled

Put the sugar, water, and ginger in a small saucepan and stir. Bring to a gentle boil over medium-high heat. Reduce the heat and simmer, stirring occasionally, until the sugar is completely dissolved and the syrup is slightly thickened, about 3 minutes.

Remove from the heat and let cool. Strain the syrup into a container with a tight-fitting lid, cover and refrigerate until ready to use. The syrup will keep, covered, in the refrigerator for up to 2 weeks.

Makes about 1 cup

SPICED SIMPLE SYRUP

This syrup, packed with cloves, star anise, cinnamon, and nutmeg is a good one to add to toddies and cider drinks.

1 cup water

8 whole cloves

1 whole star anise

Pinch of ground cinnamon

Pinch of ground nutmeg

1½ cup sugar

Put the water, cloves, star anise, cinnamon, and nutmeg in a small saucepan and stir. Bring to a gentle boil over medium-high heat. Reduce the heat and simmer for 1 minute. Add the sugar and simmer, stirring occasionally, until the sugar is completely dissolved and the syrup is slightly thickened.

Remove from the heat and let cool. Strain the syrup into a container with a tight-fitting lid, cover and refrigerate until ready to use. The syrup will keep, covered, in the refrigerator for up to 2 weeks.

Makes about 1 cup

HERBED SIMPLE SYRUP

Here's a good recipe that will brighten almost any summer cocktail. Make this syrup in season when fresh herbs such as mint, basil, and lemon verbena are in abundance.

½ cup water

1 cup sugar

1 cup chopped fresh herbs, such as mint,
   basil, sage, and lemon verbena

Put the water, sugar, and herbs in a small saucepan and stir. Bring to a gentle boil over medium-high heat. Reduce the heat and simmer, stirring occasionally, until the sugar is completely dissolved and the syrup is slightly thickened.

Remove from the heat and let cool. Strain the syrup into a container with a tight-fitting lid, cover and refrigerate until ready to use. The syrup will keep, covered, in the refrigerator for up to 2 weeks.

Makes about 1 cup

FRUIT SHRUBS

A shrub is made with fresh fruit, sugar, and vinegar and it's a wonderful, refreshing beverage either on its own or added to a drink. Fill a tall glass with ice, add a splash of your preferred shrub and a shot of whiskey, gin, or vodka and you will have a lovely summer cocktail. It's also nice to add champagne or sparkling wine to a fruit shrub.

> 1 pound chopped fruit
>
> 2 cups sugar
>
> 2 cups white wine vinegar

Put the fruit in a large nonreactive bowl. Using a muddler or the back of a spoon, mash the fruit a bit. Add the sugar and toss well to combine. Cover the mixture with plastic wrap and let it sit in the refrigerator for 2 days, stirring occasionally.

Strain the mixture through a fine mesh sieve, pressing on the solids to extract as much liquid as possible. Pour the liquid (shrub) into a clean dry container with a lid. Add the vinegar and shake vigorously to combine. Put the shrub in the refrigerator for 5 days or up to a week, shaking the jar occasionally.

The shrub will keep in the refrigerator for a few weeks. It should never be allowed to ferment or bubble. If it does, discard it.

Makes about 3 cups

fruits for shrubs

Some good fruits for shrubs are: strawberries, raspberries, blueberries, blackberries, cherries, peaches, plums, pears, and rhubarb.

When preparing a shrub, use very ripe fruit. It should be thoroughly rinsed and may be peeled and chopped.

MARINATED FRESH CHERRIES

*H*omemade marinated cherries are a fantastic garnish for all kinds of cocktails and they also taste great with ice cream or frozen yogurt.

1½ cups water

⅔ cup sugar

½ cup Pom juice

2 cups (about 1 pound) fresh sweet cherries

2 tablespoons fresh lemon juice

2 cinnamon sticks

1 teaspoon almond extract

Put the water, sugar, and juice in a saucepan. Bring to a simmer over medium-high heat, stirring, until the sugar dissolves. Add the cherries, lemon juice, cinnamon sticks, and almond extract and simmer for 10 minutes. Remove from the heat and let the cherries steep for 1 hour.

With a slotted spoon, transfer the cherries to a clean 1-quart jar, or two 1-pint jars. Strain the juice and pour over the cherries to cover. Cover with a tight lid. The cherries will keep in the refrigerator for up to 2 weeks.

Makes 1 quart

chapter 2

~~~~~~~~

CLASSIC COCKTAILS

~~~~~~~~

BRANDY ALEXANDER

This creamy cocktail—a blend of brandy, crème de cacao, and cream—is an old favorite and a perfect choice for an after-dinner drink.

> 3 tablespooons brandy
>
> 2 tablespoons dark crème de cacao
>
> 2 tablespoons half-and-half
>
> Generous pinch of ground nutmeg, for garnish

Fill a cocktail shaker half way with ice. Add the brandy, crème de cacao, and half-and-half and shake well. Strain into a martini glass, garnish with nutmeg, and serve.

Makes 1 drink

BLACK RUSSIAN

A Black Russian is a thoroughly satisfying drink to sip slowly. It's simple to make since it requires nothing more than shots of vodka and coffee liqueur poured over ice. A marinated cherry is an excellent garnish.

¼ cup vodka

3 tablespoons coffee liqueur

1 marinated cherry, for garnish

Fill a rocks glass with ice. Add the vodka and coffee liqueur and swirl. Garnish with the cherry, and serve.

Makes 1 drink

WHITE RUSSIAN

Here is another easy and delightful drink made with vodka, coffee liqueur, and a splash of half-and-half. Black and White Russians have no Russian roots, they are named so simply because they are made with vodka.

    ¼ cup vodka
    3 tablespoons coffee liqueur
    3 tablespoons half-and-half

Fill a rocks glass with ice. Add the vodka and coffee liqueur. Drizzle in the half-and-half and serve.

Makes 1 drink

DESSERT MANHATTAN

A dry Manhattan is a good drink to enjoy before dinner, but for a change of pace try a Dessert Manhattan. Made with bourbon and chocolate cherry liqueur, it's delicious to savor as an after-dinner drink.

3 tablespoons chocolate cherry liqueur

2 tablespoons bourbon

1 orange twist, for garnish

Fill a rocks glass with ice. Add the liqueur and bourbon, and stir gently to combine. Garnish with the orange twist, and serve.

Makes 1 drink

BOURBON AND COFFEE COCKTAIL

This after-dinner drink is a smooth blend of bourbon, coffee liqueur, and orange bitters. In addition to the well-known Kahlua, there are a number of other interesting coffee liqueurs on the market such as Luxardo Sambuca Cream from Italy, Patrón XO Café Dark Cocoa from Mexico, and Heering Coffee from Denmark.

> 3 tablespoons bourbon
>
> 1 tablespooon coffee liqueur
>
> 2 dashes of orange bitters
>
> 1 orange twist, for garnish

Fill a mixing glass with ice. Add the bourbon, coffee liqueur, and bitters and stir until chilled. Strain into a chilled cocktail glass, garnish with the orange twist, and serve.

Makes 1 drink

BOURBON AND BITTERS COCKTAIL

Fernet-Branca is an herbal liqueur that is made and widely consumed in Italy. Although it is bitter and may be an acquired taste for some, it is very popular, especially with those who enjoy sipping it as an after-dinner digestif. *Here it is shaken with bourbon, fresh lemon juice, and ginger-spiked simple syrup to make a bracing cocktail.*

3 tablespoons bourbon

1 tablespoon Fernet-Branca

1 tablespoon plus 1 teaspoon fresh lemon juice

1 tablespoon Ginger Simple Syrup
(see page 13)

1 dash of Angostura bitters

1 mint sprig, for garnish

Fill a cocktail shaker with ice. Add the bourbon, Fernet-Branca, lemon juice, syrup, and bitters and shake well. Strain into a rocks glass filled with ice. Garnish with the mint sprig, and serve.

Makes 1 drink

bitters

Bitters are bar ingredients that are indispensable to great cocktail making. A dash of bitters adds flavor, depth, and complexity to a number of cocktails, much as salt, pepper, and herbs do for savory dishes.

Made by a process of macerating herbs, fruit, and spices in high-proof spirits, bitters were originally created for medicinal purposes. They soon found their way into cocktails as flavor enhancers that brought a nice kick into the mix.

Along with the renaissance of crafting classic cocktails, the reemergence of bitters has followed. In addition to the essential and most commonly used bitters—Angostura, Peychaud's, and Orange—there is a huge variety and selection of bitters on the market. The options may be overwhelming, but they're definitely worth experimenting with.

DERBY DESSERT COCKTAIL

Although the official drink of the Kentucky Derby is the Mint Julep, this cocktail, sweetened with maple and ginger syrup could give it a run for the money.

¼ cup whiskey or bourbon

1 tablespoon plus 1 teaspoon grapefruit juice

1 tablespoon maple syrup

1 tablespoon Ginger Simple Syrup (see page 13)

2 dashes of Angostura bitters

1 mint sprig, for garnish

Fill a cocktail shaker with ice and add the whiskey, grapefruit juice, maple syrup, ginger syrup, and bitters. Strain into a cocktail glass, garnish with the mint sprig, and serve.

Makes 1 drink

HIGHLAND HOLIDAY COCKTAIL

This drink, with a hint of mellow smokiness, is a good one to sip on in front of the fire after a long holiday meal.

> ¼ cup scotch
>
> 2 tablespoons fresh lemon juice
>
> 1 tablespoon plus 1 teaspoon maple syrup
>
> 1 dash of Pastis
>
> Sparkling apple cider
>
> 1 apple slice, for garnish

Fill a cocktail shaker with ice. Add the scotch, lemon juice, maple syrup, and Pastis. Shake well and strain into a highball glass filled with ice. Top off with the apple cider, garnish with the apple slice, and serve.

Makes 1 drink

GRASSHOPPER

This classic after-dinner drink is made with crème de menthe, crème de cacao, and cream and is named for its color.

1 tablespoon, plus 1 teaspoon crème de menthe

1 tablespoon plus 1 teaspoon white crème de cacao

2 teaspoons heavy cream

Fill a cocktail shaker with ice. Add the crème de menthe, crème de cacao, and cream and shake vigorously. Strain into a chilled cocktail glass and serve.

Makes 1 drink

AMARETTO SOUR

This not-too-sweet version of an Amaretto Sour makes a very good after-dinner drink that pairs well with chocolate.

> 3 tablespoons amaretto
>
> 1 tablespoon plus 1 teaspoon bourbon
>
> 2 tablespoons fresh lemon juice
>
> 1 teaspoon Simple Syrup (see page 10)
>
> 1 tablespoon beaten egg white
>
> 1 lemon twist, for garnish
>
> 1 marinated cherry, for garnish

Fill a cocktail shaker with cracked ice. Add the amaretto, bourbon, lemon juice, syrup, and egg white and shake well. Strain into a rocks glass filled with ice. Garnish with the lemon twist and cherry, and serve.

Makes 1 drink

COGNAC SOUR

Although Cognac is most often thought of as a spirit to sip on its own, its unique flavor shines when it's mixed with fresh lemon juice and a bit of Simple Syrup.

> **3 tablespoons Cognac**
> **1 tablespoon fresh lemon juice**
> **1 teaspoon Simple Syrup (see page 10)**

Fill a cocktail shaker with ice. Add the Cognac, lemon juice, and syrup and shake well. Strain into a rocks glass filled with ice and serve.

Makes 1 drink

chapter 3

~~~~~~~~~~

FRESH
FRUIT
COCKTAILS

~~~~~~~~~~

FRESH LEMONADE

*H*ot summer days call for refreshing lemonade served in tall glasses over ice. This recipe, made with freshly squeezed lemons and Simple Syrup, is a snap to make and can be used as a base for a number of summery drinks.

    5 to 6 lemons

    4 cups cold water

    ¾ cup Simple Syrup (see page 10)

Squeeze the lemons to make 1 cup of fresh lemon juice. Transfer to a large container or pitcher. Add the water and syrup and stir well. Refrigerate the lemonade for at least 1 hour before serving.

Makes about 1½ quarts

FRESH LIMEADE

Limeade is another perfect summer refresher to drink on its own or to add to vodka, rum, or tequila drinks. This is on the tart side so you may want to add a bit more sugar or syrup to taste.

> **8 to 10 limes**
>
> **4 cups cold water**
>
> **¾ cup Simple Syrup or Honey Syrup**
> **(see page 10 and page 12)**

Squeeze the limes to make 1 cup of fresh lime juice. Transfer to a large container or pitcher. Add the water and syrup and stir well. Refrigerate the limeade for at least 1 hour before serving.

Makes about 1½ quarts

STRAWBERRY-CHAMPAGNE COCKTAIL

Champagne and other sparkling wines always add a festive note to any occasion and are often served before a meal. But a champagne cocktail made with a fresh strawberry shrub is lovely to sip after dinner, too.

1 teaspoon strawberry fruit shrub (see page 17)

1 teaspooon dark crème de cacao

¾ cup chilled champagne

1 small strawberry, for garnish

Pour the shrub and crème de cacao in a chilled champagne flute. Top off with champagne. Garnish with the strawberry, and serve.

Makes 1 drink

STRAWBERRY-MINT JULEP

*T*his refreshing drink is perfect to serve after a Derby Day lunch or brunch. Be sure to use the freshest mint that you can find.

3 large strawberries, hulled

8 fresh mint leaves

2 tablespoons Simple Syrup (see page 10)

¼ cup bourbon

1 cup crushed ice

1 mint sprig, for garnish

1 strawberry, halved lengthwise

Put the strawberries, mint leaves, and syrup in a rocks glass or silver julep cup and muddle together. Add the bourbon, fill the glass halfway with crushed ice and stir to combine. Fill the rest of the glass with crushed ice and stir until the glass is frosty. Add more ice if needed to fill the glass. Garnish with the mint sprig and strawberry, and serve.

Makes 1 drink

FRESH BLUEBERRY PROSECCO

Here is a simple yet sophisticated sparkler that's lovely to serve during blueberry season.

⅓ cup Simple Syrup (see page 10)

2 cups fresh or frozen blueberries, thawed if frozen

1 750-ml bottle prosecco

Fresh blueberries, for garnish

6 mint sprigs, for garnish

Put the syrup and blueberries in a blender and blend until smooth. Strain the mixture through a fine mesh sieve, pressing on the solids to extract as much liquid as possible. Discard the solids.

Spoon 2 tablespoons each into six champagne flutes. Fill the glasses with prosecco and gently stir. Garnish each drink with fresh blueberries and a mint sprig, and serve.

Makes 6 drinks

RHUBARB SHRUB

Fresh rhubarb is a sure sign of spring and this tangy cocktail made with Aperol, rhubarb shrub, and strawberry puree is a delicious dessert in a glass that celebrates the season.

3 tablespoons rosato vermouth

1 tablespoon Aperol

1 teaspoon rhubarb fruit shrub (see page 17)

1 tablespoon strawberry puree

1 teaspoon fresh lemon juice

Dash of rhubarb bitters

Fresh strawberries and blueberries, for garnish

1 mint sprig, for garnish

Confectioners' sugar, for garnish

Fill a cocktail shaker with ice and add the vermouth, Aperol, shrub, puree, lemon juice, and bitters. Shake well and strain into a stemmed glass filled with crushed ice.

Garnish with the berries and mint. Sprinkle with the sugar, and serve.

Makes 1 drink

MANGO-RUM COCKTAIL

Beautiful, fruity, tropical drinks are fun to serve after dinner since they are sweet and refreshing. When making drinks in a blender, it is best to add the ice after the fruit and spirits are blended.

3 tablespoons rum

1 tablespoon triple sec

¾ cup chopped fresh mango cubes

1½ tablespoons fresh lime juice

2 teaspoons superfine sugar

1 cup ice cubes

1 lime wheel, for garnish

Put the rum, triple sec, mangos, lime juice, and sugar in a blender and blend on low speed until smooth. Add the ice cubes and blend on higher speed until very smooth. Pour into a large stemmed glass, garnish with the lime wheel, and serve.

Makes 1 drink

FROZEN BANANA DAIQUIRI

Banana daiquiris are refreshingly rich and smooth—kind of perfect to serve for dessert.

3 tablespoons light rum

1 banana, peeled and cut into 1-inch pieces

1 tablespoon triple sec

1½ tablespoons fresh lime juice

1 teaspoon superfine sugar

1 cup crushed ice

1 whole raspberry or blackberry, for garnish

Put the rum, banana, triple sec, lime juice, and sugar in a blender and blend on low speed until smooth. Add the ice and blend on higher speed until very smooth. Pour into a large stemmed glass, garnish with the raspberry or blackberry, and serve.

Makes 1 drink

HONEYDEW MARGARITA

This drink is a fruity twist on a classic Margarita with a tantalizing sugar and salt blend for rimming the glass.

- 1 teaspoon sugar, for rimming the glass
- 1 teaspoon kosher salt, for rimming the glass
- 1 lime wedge, for rimming the glass
- 1 cup chopped honeydew melon
- ¼ cup tequila
- 2 tablespoons Grand Marnier
- 1½ tablespoons fresh lime juice
- 1 lime wheel, for garnish

Pour the sugar and salt onto a small, shallow plate. Rub the rim of a rocks glass or coupe with the lime wedge. Dip it into the sugar/salt mixture to coat the rim of the glass.

Put the melon in a blender and blend until smooth.

Fill a cocktail shaker with ice and add the pureed melon, tequila, Grand Marnier, and lime juice and shake well. Strain into the prepared glass filled with ice. Garnish with the lime wheel, and serve.

Makes 1 drink

WATERMELON-MINT COOLER

*W*atermelon is so sweet and refreshing and it's a natural to add to a cocktail. This one features blended and sliced watermelon and it is as utterly delicious as it is beautiful.

½ cup chopped and seeded watermelon

3 mint leaves

1 tablespoon Ginger Simple Syrup (see page 13)

¼ cup vodka

1 tablespoon fresh lime juice

Ginger ale

1 watermelon slice, for garnish

1 mint sprig, for garnish

Put the watermelon, mint, and syrup in a cocktail shaker and muddle. Add the vodka and lime juice and fill with ice. Shake well and strain into a rocks glass filled with fresh ice. Top with ginger ale, garnish with the watermelon slice and mint sprig, and serve.

Makes 1 drink

ADULT ARNOLD PALMER

An Arnold Palmer is made with equal parts iced tea and lemonade and was named for the world-famous golfer who was known to order it at restaurants and clubhouses. An alcoholic version of the drink is called an "Adult Arnold Palmer" or a "Tipsy Arnold Palmer". Whatever you call it, it's a lovely summery cocktail.

⅓ cup iced tea, preferably homemade

⅓ cup fresh lemonade
(see page 42)

3 tablespoons vodka

1 lemon wedge, for garnish

1 mint sprig, for garnish

Fill a large rocks glass with ice. Add the tea, lemonade, and vodka. Stir with a long spoon. Garnish with the lemon wedge and mint sprig, and serve.

Makes 1 drink

FROZEN ORANGE NEGRONI

A traditional Negroni is made with Campari, sweet vermouth, and gin and is garnished with an orange peel. This is a refreshing riff on the classic that's made with fresh orange juice, Simple Syrup, and crushed ice.

¼ cup fresh orange juice

2 tablespoons Campari

2 tablespoons gin

2 tablespoons sweet vermouth

1½ tablespoons Simple Syrup (see page 10)

¾ cup ice

1 orange wheel, for garnish

Put the orange juice, Campari, gin, vermouth, syrup, and half of the ice in a blender and blend until smooth. Add the remaining ice and blend again until very smooth. Pour into a rocks glass, garnish with the orange wheel, and serve.

Makes 1 drink

PALOMA PALETAS

Frosty ice pops are tasty summer treats. In Mexico they are called paletas. *Here's a paleta recipe that's a frozen version of a Paloma made with mezcal and fresh grapefruit and lime juices. These cool pops are a perfect dessert to serve after an outdoor barbecue.*

½ cup agave syrup

¼ cup mezcal

1½ cups fresh grapefruit juice

¼ cup fresh lime juice

Large pinch of salt

In a medium bowl, whisk together the agave syrup and mezcal. Add the grapefruit and lime juices and salt and transfer to a pitcher with a spout. Pour the mixture into six ice pop molds, dividing evenly. Transfer to a freezer and freeze until solid, about 4 hours or preferably overnight.

Makes 6 pops

APEROL SPRITZ ICE POPS

These ice pops are so pretty because of the brilliant bright colors of the Aperol and fresh orange and lemon juices.

    1½ cups water

    ⅓ cup sugar

    ½ cup prosecco

    ⅓ cup Aperol

    ¼ cup freshly squeezed orange juice

    ¼ cup freshly squeezed lemon juice

Combine the water and sugar in a small saucepan. Bring to a boil, reduce the heat, and simmer for about 2 minutes, stirring occasionally, until the sugar is completely dissolved. Set aside to cool. Add the prosecco, Aperol, orange juice and lemon juice and stir. Transfer the mixture to a pitcher with a spout. Pour the mixture into six ice pop molds, dividing evenly. Transfer to a freezer and freeze until solid, about 4 hours or preferably overnight.

Makes 6 pops

MARGARITA ICE POPS

What's better than a nice tart Margarita-flavored icy treat on a hot summer night? These pops are incredibly tasty and refreshing.

> 1⅓ cups water
>
> ¼ cup sugar
>
> 1 tablespoon fresh grated lime zest
>
> Pinch of salt
>
> ⅔ cup freshly squeezed lime juice
>
> 3 tablespoons tequila
>
> 2 tablespoons triple sec

Combine the water, sugar, lime zest, and salt in a small saucepan. Bring to a boil, reduce the heat, and simmer for about 2 minutes, stirring occasionally, until the sugar is completely dissolved. Set aside to cool. Add the lime juice, tequila, and triple sec and stir. Transfer the mixture to a pitcher with a spout. Pour the mixture into six ice pop molds, dividing evenly. Transfer to a freezer and freeze until solid, about 4 hours or preferably overnight.

Makes 6 pops

~~~~~~~~~

chapter 4

GRANITAS, AFFOGATOS & ICE CREAM DRINKS

~~~~~~~~~

granitas

A granita is a frozen dessert made with sugar, water, and assorted flavors. It is usually made with fruit, coffee, or tea and is excellent with an added aperitivo or liqueur. Granitas need at least 3 or 4 hours in the freezer and several good stirs to reach their consistency, so plan accordingly.

MINT JULEP GRANITA

This is made with its own simple syrup infused with fresh mint. Use more or fewer leaves depending on your taste.

1½ cups water

¾ cup sugar

1 cup fresh mint leaves, plus more for garnish

¼ cup bourbon

1 teaspoon crème de menthe

Put the water and sugar and in a medium saucepan. Bring to a boil, reduce the heat and cook, stirring, until the sugar is dissolved, 1 to 2 minutes. Remove from the heat and stir in the mint leaves. Let cool to room temperature, transfer to the refrigerator and chill for at least 30 minutes.

Strain the syrup into a 9-by-13-inch baking dish or metal pan, cover with plastic wrap, and transfer to a level shelf in the freezer. Using a fork, stir the mixture every 30 minutes, scraping the edges and breaking up any ice chunks, until the granita is slushy and frozen, about 3 hours.

To serve, scoop the granita into chilled glasses, garnish with mint leaves, and serve.

Makes 4 servings

COFFEE GRANITA

A coffee granita made with coffee liqueur and topped with ice cream or whipped cream is a delightful hot weather treat. You'll want to make it all summer!

2 cups espresso or strong black coffee,
   at room temperature

½ cup sugar

2 tablespoons coffee liqueur

1 tablespoon grated lemon zest

Whipped cream (optional), for serving

Ice cream (optional), for serving

Put the espresso, sugar, liqueur, and lemon zest in a pitcher and stir together until the sugar melts. Pour the mixture into a 9-by-13-inch baking dish or metal pan, cover with plastic wrap, and transfer to a level shelf in the freezer. Using a fork, stir the mixture every 30 minutes, scraping the edges and breaking up any ice chunks, until the granita is slushy and frozen, about 3 hours.

To serve, scoop the granita into chilled glasses and top with whipped cream or ice cream, if desired.

Makes 4 servings

CAMPARI AND GRAPEFRUIT GRANITA

What could be more refreshing than a granita made with fresh grapefruit juice and Campari? This slightly bitter, icy treat is an excellent palate cleanser.

2 cups freshly squeezed grapefruit juice

½ cup Campari

½ cup sugar

⅓ cup water

4 mint sprigs, for garnish

Put the grapefruit juice, Campari, and sugar, and water in a blender and purée until smooth. Pour into a 9-by-13-inch baking dish or a metal pan, cover with plastic wrap, and transfer to a level shelf in the freezer. Using a fork, stir the mixture every 30 minutes, scraping the edges and breaking up any ice chunks, until the granita is slushy and frozen, about 3 hours.

To serve, scoop the granita into chilled glasses, garnish with the mint sprigs, and serve.

Makes 4 servings

affogatos

An *affogato* is a combination of a scoop of
ice cream and a shot of espresso. The Italian
translation for *affogato* means drowned,
normally a bad thing. But there is nothing
more delicious than an affogato with a shot
of espresso and something stronger.

CHOCOLATE AND AMARETTO AFFOGATO

*A*lmond-flavored amaretto, espresso, and chocolate are a fabulous and decadent combination in this affogato.

- 4 scoops of chocolate ice cream
- 4 shots espresso
- ¼ cup amaretto
- 4 ounces chocolate, shaved

Scoop the ice cream into four latte glasses or coupes. Pour the espresso and amaretto over each serving. Garnish with the shaved chocolate, and serve at once.

Makes 4 servings

NOCINO AFFOGATO

*N*ocino is an Italian spirit infused with green walnuts. It is traditionally sipped as a digestif on its own, but because of its rich and spicy flavor it is often found in dessert drinks.

    4 scoops of vanilla ice cream

    4 shots espresso

    ¼ cup Nocino

Scoop the ice cream into four latte glasses or coupes. Pour the espresso and Nocino over the ice cream and serve at once.

Makes 4 servings

AFFOGRONI

If blood orange sorbet isn't available, lemon sorbet or vanilla ice cream are also very good to use in this delicious dessert.

  4 scoops of blood orange sorbet
  ¼ cup Campari
  ¼ cup Aperol

Scoop the sorbet into four latte glasses or coupes. Pour the Campari and Aperol over the sorbet and serve at once.

Makes 4 servings

campari and aperol

Campari and Aperol are both wonderful spirits to stock in your home bar. These aperitivos have unique, bitter flavors and are most often served before meals. They're also zesty and delicious additions to desserts like granitas, affogatos, and ice pops.

Campari is an Italian aperitif that was created by Gaspare Campari in 1860 in the town of Novara, Italy. It is made from secret infusion of bitter herbs, fruit, and plants in water and alcohol. With its deep, rich, red color and distinctive bitter taste that some say is an acquired one, Campari is the star ingredient of many iconic cocktails such as the Negroni, the Americano, and the Boulevardier.

Like Campari, Aperol is made from a secret recipe of infusions that include sweet and bitter oranges, rhubarb, and a mix of herbs and roots. It originated in Padua, Italy, in 1919. Aperol is bright orange and tastes a bit lighter and sweeter than Campari.

RUM-SPIKED HORCHATA

Horchata is a sweet milk drink made with pulverized uncooked rice. This refreshing agua fresca is very popular in Mexico and other Latin American countries and is especially good with a healthy dose of rum.

1 pound of uncooked long-grain rice

6 cups cold water

Generous pinch of ground cinnamon,
   plus more for garnish

⅓ cup sugar

1 teaspoon vanilla

½ cup light rum

4 cinnamon sticks, for garnish

The day before serving, soak the rice in 3 cups of the water overnight. Transfer the rice, soaking water, and cinnamon to a blender and puree until smooth.

Strain the mixture into a pitcher through a fine-mesh sieve or several layers of cheesecloth. Add 3 cups of water, sugar, and vanilla and stir well. Taste and adjust the flavors, if necessary.

To serve, fill four large glasses with ice and add the rum in equal parts. Pour horchata into each glass and stir with a long spoon. Garnish each drink with the cinnamon and a cinnamon stick, and serve.

Makes 4 servings

THIN MINT COCKTAIL

*T*hin mints are a favorite among Girl Scout cookie aficionados, so this dessert cocktail made with a blend of crème de menthe and chocolate ice cream is sure to please your cookie-loving guests.

> 1 pint chocolate ice cream
>
> 1 cup cold whole milk
>
> ¼ cup crème de menthe
>
> 2 tablespoons vodka
>
> 1 cup ice
>
> Chocolate shavings, for garnish
>
> 4 fresh mint sprigs, for garnish

Put the ice cream, milk, crème de menthe, and vodka in a blender. Blend until very smooth. Add the ice and blend again until smooth. Pour into four rocks glasses, garnish with the chocolate shavings and mint sprigs, and serve.

Makes 4 servings

ROOT BEER-BOURBON ICE CREAM FLOAT

*R*oot beer and vanilla ice cream are a classic combination for one of America's favorite floats. When you add a shot of bourbon to the mix you have a deliciously boozy ice cream extravaganza.

> 1 cup bourbon
>
> Three 12-ounce bottles of root beer, chilled
>
> 1 pint vanilla ice cream

Divide the bourbon evenly among four chilled glasses or mugs. Add equal amounts of the root beer to the glasses and gently stir. Add the ice cream to each serving. Serve at once with straws and spoons.

Makes 4 servings

BERRY-PROSECCO
ICE CREAM FLOAT

Summer entertaining should always be easy and this simple, elegant dessert, which features the season's best fresh berries, is lovely to serve.

> 1 pint of mixed berries, such as strawberries, raspberries, and blueberries
>
> 1 tablespoon sugar
>
> 1 pint vanilla ice cream
>
> 1 750-ml bottle of prosecco

Put the berries in a nonreactive bowl. Add the sugar, toss gently, and let the berries macerate for 30 minutes.

Divide the berries among four glasses. Top the berries with ice cream and pour the prosecco over each serving. Serve at once.

Makes 4 servings

FRENCH SORBET

This tart and fizzy dessert is divine and can be served with biscotti or your favorite cookies.

½ cup Cognac

¼ cup kirsch

1 pint lemon sorbet

1 750-ml bottle of champagne

4 lemon twists, for garnish

Divide the Cognac and kirsch among four champagne coupes. Add a generous scoop of sorbet to each dish and stir together. Fill the glasses with champagne, garnish with the lemon twists, and serve.

Makes 4 servings

chapter 5

~~~~~~~~~~

HOT TODDIES, CIDER & CHOCOLATE DRINKS

~~~~~~~~~~

HOT RUM TODDY

*D*rinking *a hot toddy on a cold night is a great way to banish the winter blues. Here is a very simple recipe for a warm and cozy cocktail that may also have medicinal powers to relieve colds and sniffles.*

> 1 cup water
>
> ¼ cup dark rum
>
> 2 tablespoons Honey Simple Syrup (see page 12)
>
> 1 tablespoon fresh lemon juice
>
> 2 lemon twists, for garnish

Boil the water and pour equal amounts into two Irish coffee glasses or heatproof mugs. Add equal parts of the rum, syrup, and lemon juice to each drink and stir. Garnish with the lemon twists, and serve.

Makes 2 drinks

APPLE-BOURBON HOT TODDY

Apple cider and bourbon are a smooth and delicious combination. This spicy cocktail, garnished with whipped cream, is a perfect way to welcome the autumn season.

1½ cups apple cider

1 tablespoon brown sugar

½ teaspoon ground nutmeg

1 vanilla bean, split

One 2-inch piece orange zest

¼ cup bourbon

Whipped cream (see page 111), for garnish

Combine the apple cider, brown sugar, nutmeg, vanilla bean, and orange zest in a medium saucepan over medium heat and simmer for 10 minutes. Pour equal amounts into two Irish coffee glasses or heatproof mugs and top each drink with the bourbon. Garnish with whipped cream, and serve.

Makes 2 drinks

HOT CIDER WITH TEQUILA

Tequila and warm cider pack a potent punch in this orange-scented after-dinner drink.

1½ cups apple cider

1 cinnamon stick

6 whole cloves

1 large piece of orange peel

¼ cup tequila

¼ cup heavy cream

Freshly grated nutmeg, for garnish

2 cinnamon sticks, for garnish

Heat the cider in a medium saucepan over low heat and bring to a simmer. Add the cinnamon stick, cloves, and orange peel and simmer for 10 minutes.

Pour equal amounts of the cider mixture and tequila into two Irish coffee glasses or heatproof mugs. Float each drink with the heavy cream on top of the cider. Garnish with the nutmeg and cinnamon sticks, and serve.

Makes 2 drinks

WARM RUM RAISIN CIDER

For a sweet and lovely nightcap, serve this spicy cider laced with dark rum. Don't forget a plate of ginger cookies.

½ tablespoon butter

½ teaspoon sugar

¼ cup golden raisins

2 whole cloves

1 cinnamon stick

2 cups apple cider

¼ cup dark rum

2 apple slices, for garnish

2 cinnamon sticks, for garnish

In a large saucepan, heat the butter over medium heat. Add the sugar, raisins, cloves, and cinnamon sticks. Cook, stirring constantly, until the sugar has caramelized, about 5 minutes.

Add the cider and heat, stirring, until the mixture just begins to simmer. Remove from the heat, stir in the rum, and ladle into two heatproof mugs or cups. Garnish with the apple slices and cinnamon sticks, and serve.

Makes 2 drinks

MEXICAN SPICE HOT CHOCOLATE

Chile liqueur is definitely worth seeking out. Made from ancho chiles steeped in a sugar cane spirit, it adds a sweet and smoky flavor to all kinds of drinks, including homemade hot chocolate.

1½ cups whole milk

2 tablespoons unsweetened cocoa powder

2 ounces unsweetened chocolate, chopped

2 tablespoons sugar

1 star anise pod

1 vanilla bean, split

Pinch of cayenne pepper

Pinch of salt

¼ cup tequila

1 tablespoon ancho chili liqueur, such as Ancho Reyes

2 orange twists, for garnish

Combine the milk, cocoa powder, and chocolate in a medium saucepan and cook over low heat, stirring, until the chocolate melts. Add the sugar, star anise, vanilla bean, cayenne pepper, and salt. Reduce the heat and simmer for 10 minutes.

Strain the mixture into two coffee mugs or cups and stir in equal parts of the tequila and chili liqueur. Garnish with the orange twists, and serve.

Makes 2 drinks

cooking with chocolate

When you're preparing homemade hot chocolate, it's always preferable to use good-quality baking chocolate or chocolate chips instead of the instant powdered type or overly sweet chocolate syrup. Chocolate is sold in many forms, from large bars to 1-ounce squares to ½-inch chunks and mini chips. If the chocolate is sweetened, it will be called bittersweet, semisweet, or sweet, depending on the amount of sugar and how it's made. If you're cooking with chocolate squares or chunks, they should be chopped into very small pieces for melting. It's best to use a large chef's knife instead of a food processor to do this.

Because all chocolate scorches easily and its flavor can be ruined, be careful when adding it to warm milk. The milk should come to a very low simmer over low heat and it should never boil before or after adding chocolate.

AMARETTO HOT CHOCOLATE

Italian for "a little bitter," amaretto is a very popular after-dinner drink and coffee enhancer. This liqueur's rich nutty flavor also pairs beautifully with hot chocolate.

> 2 cups whole milk
>
> 4 ounces semisweet chocolate, chopped
>
> ½ teaspoon vanilla extract
>
> ¼ cup amaretto
>
> Whipped cream (see page 111), for garnish
>
> Chocolate shavings, for garnish

Heat half of the milk in a medium saucepan over low heat. Add the chocolate, stirring constantly, until melted. Raise the heat to medium and whisk in the remaining milk. Do not allow the mixture to boil. Stir in the vanilla.

Pour the hot chocolate into two coffee mugs or cups and stir in equal parts of the amaretto. Garnish with the whipped cream and chocolate shavings, and serve.

Makes 2 drinks

HOT CHOCOLATE AND PEPPERMINT SCHNAPPS

Here's a great recipe for an easy and fun holiday dessert. The peppermint flavor really shines through in these festive cups of cheer.

2 cups whole milk

4 ounces semisweet chocolate, chopped

¼ cup peppermint schnapps

Whipped cream (see page 111), for garnish

2 peppermint sticks or candy canes, for garnish

Heat half of the milk in a medium saucepan over low heat. Add the chocolate, stirring constantly, until melted. Raise the heat to medium and whisk in the remaining milk. Do not allow the mixture to boil.

Pour the hot chocolate into two coffee mugs or cups and stir in equal parts of the peppermint schnapps. Garnish with the whipped cream and peppermint sticks, and serve.

Makes 2 drinks

chapter 6

~~~~~~~~~~~~

COFFEE COCKTAILS
& DRINKS

~~~~~~~~~~~~

CREAMY SPIKED ICED COFFEE

*H*ere is a perfect example of a strong cold coffee cocktail
that also acts as a dessert.

　　½ cup cold black coffee

　　3 tablespoons vanilla vodka

　　2 tablespoons coffee liqueur

　　1 tablespoon heavy cream

Fill a cocktail shaker with ice. Add the coffee, vodka,
coffee liqueur, and cream and shake vigorously. Strain
into a tall glass filled with ice and serve.

Makes 1 drink

ESPRESSO MARTINI

This sophisticated after-dinner drink is a potent mix of strong espresso, vodka, coffee liqueur, and white crème de cacao.

2 tablespoons cold espresso

3 tablespoons vodka

1 tablespoon coffee liqueur

1 tablespoon white crème de cacao

Fill a cocktail shaker with ice. Add the espresso, vodka, coffee liqueur, and crème de cacao and shake well. Strain into a chilled martini glass and serve.

Makes 1 drink

CLASSIC IRISH COFFEE

There are a few rules when it comes to making traditional Irish coffee, but the most important one is to always use Irish whiskey.

   ¾ cup hot black coffee

   2 tablespoons Irish whiskey

   2 teaspoons sugar

   Heavy cream

Pour the coffee and whiskey into a warmed Irish coffee glass. Add the sugar and stir to dissolve. Float the cream on top and serve.

Makes 1 drink

CREAMY IRISH COFFEE

*H*ere is a sweeter, creamier version of the classic. It's garnished with a cloud of freshly whipped cream and a generous sprinkling of cocoa powder.

2 tablespoons Irish whiskey

1 tablespoon Simple Syrup (see page 10)

¾ cup hot black coffee

Whipped cream (see page 111), for garnish

Unsweetened cocoa powder, for garnish

Pour the whiskey and syrup into a warmed Irish coffee glass and stir. Pour the coffee into the glass until it's about three-quarters full. Top with a generous dollop of whipped cream, dust with the cocoa powder, and serve.

Makes 1 drink

SALT CARAMEL COFFEE

This blend of salty-sweet caramel sauce and coffee with a touch of cocoa and rum is an indulgent after-dinner delight.

½ cup whole milk

2 tablespoons salted caramel sauce,
   plus more for garnish

1 teaspoon unsweetened cocoa powder

¾ cup hot black coffee

2 tablespoons dark rum

Whipped cream (see page 111), for garnish

Combine the milk, caramel sauce, and cocoa powder in a small saucepan. Heat over low heat until warm, stirring well until the powder is dissolved.

Add the coffee and rum and stir again. Pour into a coffee mug or cup, garnish with whipped cream, drizzle with additional caramel sauce, and serve.

Makes 1 drink

CAFFÈ CORRETTO

Caffè corretto literally means "corrected coffee" in Italian and it is often served as a hair-of-the-dog drink in Italy. It consists of a shot of espresso with a shot of liquor like sweet grappa, brandy, or Sambuca. Caffè Corretto is also good to serve after dinner. Bring a variety of liqueurs to the table and let your guests choose their own to add to espresso.

> 1 cup hot espresso
>
> 1 tablespoon grappa, brandy, or Sambuca
>
> 1 teaspoon sugar
>
> 1 lemon twist, for garnish

Pour the espresso into an espresso cup. Add the liqueur and the sugar and stir well. Garnish with the lemon twist, and serve.

Makes 1 drink

BRANDIED MOCHA COFFEE

*B*r*andy-laced, chocolate-flavored coffee always hits the spot. This is a delightful after-dinner drink.*

½ cup whole milk

1 teaspoon unsweetened cocoa powder

1½ teaspoons sugar

2 teaspoons brandy

¾ cup hot black coffee

Whipped cream (see page 111), for garnish

In a medium saucepan, heat the milk over medium heat. Add the the cocoa powder and sugar and stir until they are dissolved and the mixture is steaming but not boiling. Stir in the brandy.

Slowly pour the hot coffee into the milk mixture, stirring constantly. Pour into a large coffee mug or cup, garnish with the whipped cream, and serve.

Makes 1 drink

FRESH WHIPPED CREAM

Here is a simple recipe for basic whipped cream. Be sure not to over-whip the cream: you want it to have a light and fluffy texture.

1 cup heavy cream, chilled

2 tablespoons sugar

1 teaspoon vanilla extract

In a medium bowl with an electric mixer on high speed, whip the cream, sugar, and vanilla just until stiff peaks begin to form. If not using right away, cover with plastic wrap and refrigerate until ready to serve, up to 1 day. If the cream is separated, whisk again to its proper consistency before serving.

Makes about 2 cups

chapter 7

LIGHT
DESSERT BITES

LINZER HEART COOKIES

*W*hen making these beautiful cookies, be sure that the nuts are very finely chopped in the food processor so the dough will roll out smoothly. You will need a graduated set of heart-shaped cookies cutters to make these.

1 cup unblanched almonds

2¼ cups unbleached all-purpose flour

¾ teaspoon ground cinnamon

¼ teaspoon salt

1 cup (2 sticks) unsalted butter, at room temperature

¾ cup confectioners' sugar, plus extra for dusting

2 large egg yolks, at room temperature

1 teaspoon lemon zest

About ¾ cup strawberry or raspberry seedless
   preserves, at room temperature

Combine the almonds and ½ cup of the flour in a food processor and pulse until the nuts are very finely ground. Add the remaining 1¾ cups of flour, cinnamon, and salt and pulse until thoroughly mixed.

In a large bowl with an electric mixer set on medium speed, beat the butter and sugar until light and fluffy, about 2–3 minutes. Scrape down the sides of the bowl as needed. Add the egg yolks one at a time, beating well after each addition. Beat in the lemon zest. With the mixer set on low speed, beat in the flour mixture in 3 additions to combine.

Divide the dough into quarters, shape each quarter into a disk, and wrap individually in plastic wrap. Refrigerate the dough for 1–2 hours. (The dough can be refrigerated for up to 1 day. Let stand at room temperature for about 10 minutes to soften slightly before rolling.)

Position the oven racks in the top third and center of the oven and preheat the oven to 350°F.

On a well-floured surface, using a floured rolling pin, roll out one piece of the dough about ⅛-inch thick. Cut out cookies with a 2½-inch heart-shaped cutter and, using a metal spatula, transfer the cookies to an ungreased baking sheet, spacing them about 1 inch apart. Wrap the remaining dough scraps in plastic and refrigerate. Roll out the second piece of dough, cut out more cookies, and transfer to another ungreased baking sheet. Using a ¾-to 1-inch heart-shaped cutter, cut out the centers of the cookies on the second baking sheet. Add the cut out centers to the dough scraps.

Bake the cookies for 9–12 minutes, switching the position of the baking sheets halfway through baking, until the edges are just starting to brown. The cookies with cutouts will take slightly less time to bake than the whole cookies. Let cool on baking sheets for about 1 minute, then transfer the cookies to wire racks to cool completely. Repeat with the remaining dough then reroll the scraps to make more cookies, keeping in mind that you want an equal amount of whole and cut-out cookies.

To assemble the cookies: Spread a bit of preserves evenly over the top of each whole cookie. Dust the tops of the cut-out cookies with the sugar and place them over the whole cookies. The cookies can be stored between layers of waxed paper in an airtight container for up to 5 days.

Makes about 34 sandwich cookies

RAISIN-WALNUT BISCOTTI

*B*iscotti —*Italian biscuits or cookies —are intensely crunchy, which makes them perfect for dunking into coffee, tea, or dessert wine.*

2 cups unbleached all-purpose flour

2 teaspoons baking powder

1 teaspoon ground cinnamon

¼ cup (½ stick) unsalted butter,
   at room temperature

⅔ cup sugar

2 large eggs, at room temperature

1 teaspoon vanilla extract

1 cup walnuts, toasted and chopped

1 cup golden raisins

Position an oven rack in the center of the oven and preheat the oven to 350°F. Grease a large baking sheet.

In a large bowl, whisk the flour, baking powder, and cinnamon together. In another large bowl, using an electric mixer set on low speed, beat the butter, sugar, eggs and vanilla together. Add the flour mixture and stir until just combined. Add the raisins and walnuts and stir to blend.

Divide the dough in half. Shape each half into a long loaf, about 16-by-2-inches each. Arrange the loaves on the prepared baking sheet and flatten them slightly.

Bake until lightly browned, about 20 minutes. Transfer to racks and let cool.

With a serrated knife, cut the loaves diagonally into ¾-inch slices. Arrange the slices, cut-side down, onto a clean baking sheet and bake them for 6 minutes a side, until lightly browned. Remove and let cool on a rack.

Makes about 30 biscotti

LEMON WAFERS

These crisp cookies are delicious with ice cream or sorbet; they're also perfect for dipping into coffee. They keep beautifully in an airtight container until ready to serve.

6 tablespoons unsalted butter, at room temperature

1 cup sugar

1 large egg, at room temperature

1¼ cups unbleached all-purpose flour

½ cup almonds, ground

Position an oven rack in the center of the oven and preheat the oven to 350°F. Lightly butter two baking sheets.

In a large bowl with an electric mixer set on medium speed, beat the butter, sugar, and egg until smooth. Stir in the flour, almonds, and lemon juice and mix until well combined.

Spoon the dough onto the prepared baking sheets and then press the dough into 2½-inch rounds with floured fingers.

Bake until the edges of the cookies are lightly browned, 10–12 minutes. Remove the cookies with a spatula and cool on racks.

Makes 2 dozen cookies

GINGER COOKIES

Beautifully spiced with ginger, cinnamon, and cloves, these delicious cookies are the perfect bite to accompany coffee, espresso, or tea.

2 cups unbleached all-purpose flour

1½ teaspoons baking soda

½ teaspoon salt

1 tablespoon ground ginger

1½ teaspoons ground cinnamon

½ teaspoon ground cloves

1 cup sugar, plus more for rolling

¾ cup (1½ sticks) unsalted butter, softened

1 large egg

¼ cup dark molasses

Position an oven rack in the center of the oven and preheat the oven to 350°F. Lightly butter two baking sheets.

Combine the flour, baking soda, salt, ginger, cinnamon, and cloves in a bowl and whisk together to combine.

In a large bowl, with an electric mixer set on medium speed, beat the sugar and butter together. Add the egg and beat until fluffy. Add the molasses and beat to mix. Add the dry ingredients to the batter and beat until smooth.

Spread sugar in a shallow dish. Roll walnut-sized pieces of dough between lightly greased palms into 1½-inch balls. Roll each ball in the sugar to coat, and transfer to the baking sheets, leaving about 1½-inches between the cookies. Bake for 10–12 minutes or until the cookies spread and the tops crack. Cool on wire racks.

Makes about 30 cookies

CHOCOLATE MERINGUE DROPS

These lighter-than-air meringues are fairly easy to make, once you get the hang of it. Here are a few tips: Be sure to have all of your ingredients ready to assemble and give the meringues plenty of time to cool in the oven.

½ cup confectioners' sugar, plus more for garnish

⅓ cup unsweetened cocoa powder

5 large egg whites, at room temperature

¼ teaspoon cream of tartar

⅔ cup granulated sugar

1 teaspoon vanilla extract

¼ cup semisweet chocolate mini-chips

Position an oven rack in the center of the oven and pre-heat the oven to 300°F. Line two large baking sheets with parchment paper.

Sift the confectioners' sugar and cocoa together and set aside.

Put the egg whites and cream of tartar in a large bowl and with an electric mixer set on high speed, beat until soft peaks form. Gradually add in the sugar mixture, 1 tablespoon at a time, beating until stiff peaks form. Add the vanilla and beat until combined. Fold in the chocolate chips.

Drop the meringues by rounded tablespoons onto the prepared baking sheets to form mounds. Bake for 30 minutes, rotating the baking sheets after 15 minutes. Turn the oven off and let the meringues cool in the oven until dry, about 1 hour. Sprinkle evenly with some more confectioners' sugar. Remove the cookies carefully from the paper and serve.

Makes 3 dozen cookies

CHOCOLATE RUM BALLS

This recipe for rum balls has been a holiday favorite for years. These treats are delightfully nutty and boozy, making them perfect bites for dessert.

2½ cups crushed vanilla wafers

½ cup pecans, finely chopped

½ cup walnuts, finely chopped

1 cup confectioners' sugar, plus more for rolling

2 tablespoons unsweetened cocoa powder

¼ cup dark rum

¼ cup light corn syrup

2 tablespoons water

In a large bowl, combine the vanilla wafers, pecans, walnuts, confectioners' sugar, and cocoa powder.

In a small bowl, whisk the rum, corn syrup, and
2 tablespoons of water together until combined. Stir into
the wafer mixture until well combined. Shape into 1-inch
balls and roll in the confectioners' sugar.

Chill the rum balls for at least 2 hours. They will keep,
covered, in an airtight container for up to 3–4 weeks.

Makes about 3 dozen balls

STRAWBERRIES AND CREAM

U se the ripest, fresh strawberries that you can find when making this heavenly dessert.

STRAWBERRIES

1½ pounds strawberries, hulled and halved

¼ cup superfine sugar

¼ cup Cognac

½ teaspoon almond extract

Pinch of kosher salt

MASCARPONE CREAM

1½ cups mascarpone cream, softened

6 tablespoons heavy cream

2 tablespoons granulated sugar

Pinch kosher salt

½ cup toasted sliced almonds, for garnish

Confectioners' sugar, for garnish

For the strawberries: Put the strawberries in a large nonreactive bowl. Add the sugar, Cognac, almond extract, and salt and toss gently to coat. Cover with plastic wrap and let sit at room temperature for about 2 hours, tossing the strawberries after an hour.

For the mascarpone: In a medium bowl, whisk the mascarpone cheese with the cream, sugar, and salt until smooth.

Spoon the strawberries into bowls, top each serving with mascarpone cream, garnish with almonds, sprinkle with sugar, and serve.

Makes 6 servings

whipped cream variations

Feel free to add other tasty ingredients to
the whipped cream recipe on page 111. These
flavorings can be added to the whipped cream
when you beat in the sugar and vanilla.

Coffee Whipped Cream: Add 2 teaspoons espresso
powder and a bit more sugar, if necessary, to
the whipped cream.

Cocoa Whipped Cream: Mix 1 tablespoon
unsweetened cocoa powder and 2 teaspoons
sugar together with 2 tablespoons heavy cream to
form a thick paste. Stir into the whipped cream.

Cinnamon Whipped Cream: Add 1 teaspoon ground
cinnamon and a bit more sugar, if necessary, to
the whipped cream.

Whipped Cream with Spirits: Add 2 tablespoons
bourbon or rum to the whipped cream.

GRILLED PEACHES WITH ICE CREAM AND PROSECCO

Grilled fruit is lovely to serve after an alfresco dinner on the grill. By the time the coals burn down to a dull red with a thick covering of ash, dinner will be over and you and your guests will be in the mood for a light dessert. Grilled peaches are sweet and slightly smoky tasting, and the perfect foil for a scoop of vanilla ice cream and a drizzle of prosecco.

6 large peaches, peeled, pitted, and halved

2 tablespoons fresh lemon juice

Vanilla ice cream, for serving

Prosecco or other sparkling wine, for serving

Prepare a gas or charcoal grill. Lightly oil the grill rack to prevent sticking. If using charcoal, let the coals burn until medium hot so that they are covered with a thick layer of gray ash and are glowing red. If using a gas grill, heat it to medium-low.

Toss the peach halves with lemon juice. Lay the peaches, cut sides down, on the grill and cook for about 5 minutes, until the cut sides are golden. Turn and cook for 3-5 minutes longer, until heated through.

Serve the peaches with ice cream and pour a bit of prosecco over each serving.

Note: Once the peaches are tossed with the lemon juice, they can be held in the refrigerator for 2-3 hours, until you are ready to grill them.

Makes 6 servings

FRESH FRUIT WITH
NUTELLA DIPPING SAUCE

For an easy and festive dessert, dip pieces of assorted fresh fruits, such as strawberries, kiwi, mangos, papaya, bananas, and oranges, into this scrumptious chocolate-hazelnut dipping sauce. You can also serve bite-sized pieces of pound cake or angel food cake as additional dippers. This delicious sauce is simple to prepare and can be made up to a week ahead of time.

NUTELLA DIPPING SAUCE

1½ cup (16 ounces) chocolate syrup

½ cup chocolate hazelnut spread, such as Nutella

Fresh strawberries, rinsed

Kiwis, mangoes, and papayas, peeled, halved,
   and cut into ½-inch-thick slices

Bananas, peeled and cut into ½-inch rounds

Seedless oranges, peeled and sectioned

Pound cake or angel food cake, cut into
   bite-sized pieces (optional)

To make the sauce: In a small saucepan, stir the chocolate syrup and chocolate hazelnut spread together over low heat until smooth and warm. The sauce will keep, covered, in the refrigerator for up to 1 week. Serve warm or at room temperature.

To serve, arrange a bowl of the chocolate sauce in the center of a large platter or tray. Arrange the fruit and cake, if using, around the sauce. Serve with long toothpicks or fondue forks.

Makes 6 to 8 servings

PORT-ROASTED FIGS WITH CRÈME FRAÎCHE AND HONEY

Here is a simple and elegant dessert recipe that makes great use of sweet, luscious figs that are in season in late summer and early fall. They are roasted and then topped with crème fraîche and honey. Mascarpone, ricotta, or goat cheese can also be used instead of crème fraîche.

9 ripe fresh figs

1 cup port

6 tablespoons crème fraîche

Honey, for drizzling

Preheat the oven to 350°F.

Cut the figs lengthwise and trim the stems. Pour ½ cup of the port into a nonreactive baking dish and put the figs, cut sides up, in one layer in the dish. Pour the remaining half cup of port over the figs. Roast the figs, occasionally spooning with the port, until softened, about 30 minutes. Remove and let cool a bit.

Top each fig half with a teaspoon of crème fraîche and a drizzle of honey. Serve warm.

Makes 6 servings

Index by Recipe Name

Index by Spirits

Bluestreak Books is an imprint of Weldon Owen
a Bonnier Publishing USA company
www.bonnierpublishingusa.com

Library of Congress Cataloging in Publication data is available.
ISBN: 978-1-68188-284-0

First Printed in 2018
10 9 8 7 6 5 4 3 2 1
2018 2019 2020 2021

Printed in China